J 001.4 CEF
Cefrey, Holly.
Researching people, places
  and events

DATE DUE

JAN 2, 2013		
GAYLORD		PRINTED IN U.S.A.

EAGLE PUBLIC LIBRARY DIST.
BOX 240 EAGLE, CO 81631
(970) 328-8800

EAGLE VALLEY LIBRARY DISTRICT

1 06 0004819428

DIGITAL AND INFORMATION LITERACY ™

RESEARCHING PEOPLE, PLACES, AND EVENTS

HOLLY CEFREY

rosen publishing's
rosen central ®

New York

To Nick, Iris, and team

Published in 2010 by The Rosen Publishing Group, Inc.
29 East 21st Street, New York, NY 10010

Copyright © 2010 by The Rosen Publishing Group, Inc.

First Edition

All rights reserved. No part of this book may be reproduced in any form without permission in writing from the publisher, except by a reviewer.

Library of Congress Cataloging-in-Publication Data

Cefrey, Holly.
Researching people, places, and events / Holly Cefrey.—1st ed.
    p. cm.—(Digital and information literacy)
Includes bibliographical references and index.
ISBN-13: 978-1-4358-5317-1 (library binding)
1. Internet research—Juvenile literature. 2. Research—Methodology—Juvenile literature. 3. Report writing—Juvenile literature. I. Title.
ZA4228.C44 2010
001.4'202854678—dc22

                                                            2008046785

Manufactured in the United States of America

CPSIA Compliance Information: Batch #WR902021YA For Further Information contact Rosen Publishing, New York, New York at 1-800-237-9932

EAGLE PUBLIC LIBRARY DIST.
BOX 240 EAGLE, CO 81631
(970) 328-8800

CONTENTS

INTRODUCTION

Students write a lot of essays and reports throughout the academic year. Even after graduation from school, writing "assignments" continue through activities in businesses and communities. Writing activities like these require that a person become very familiar with a topic, very quickly.

If a topic is really interesting to the public, many sources, such as newspapers and Web sites, will offer their reports. With the ease of Web publishing, hundreds of reports can circulate within seconds, minutes, and hours. Electronic sources compete against each other to offer all there is to know on a topic. Sometimes, this means sacrificing hard facts for unproven "facts."

Every topic has known facts or established details. If something can be proven, it's considered a fact. Every topic also has details that haven't been proven to be true. Many unproven details can be spotted by the phrase, "It has been reported that . . ." This means that somewhere at some point, someone said something. What was stated was believable enough to repeat but has not yet been substantiated or proven true.

The task as an essay writer begins in researching these details. The writer will have to sift through them, whether fact or fiction. The quickest way to sift through details is to evaluate all of the sources and trim the fat.

Some sources are more valid than others. Some sources should never be used to research facts. The essay writer needs to be savvy enough to separate trusted sources from untrustworthy ones. A trusted source is an authority on a subject or a professional in the field. It can be a government, university, foundation, or museum site. It can also be a company's or individual's Web site, so long as the details can be found elsewhere. The details should also be cited, or credited from the original source.

If the source from where someone is getting his or her facts can't be traced, it shouldn't be trusted. Using this rule, this book will help the budding essay writer navigate the world of details to become a cybersleuth on people, places, and events.

Chapter 1

Search Basics

T he Web is a vast resource for research. Google has a system that tracks new URLs. Each URL leads to a Web page or site. A Web site may be a single page, have a few pages, or have thousands of pages. Some URLs lead directly to multimedia downloads like music or movie files. According to Google's official blog, the system counted over a trillion URLs in 2008. The system found 1,000,000,000,000 unique addresses on the Web—that's a huge amount of data!

These enormous resources are made available through the browser, which is an application, or program, that gives a computer instructions to carry out tasks. It allows surfers to interact with the many collections of text, images, movies, and interactive data on the Web. The surfer simply types the address of the desired Web site in the browser's address field and hits return. Almost instantly, the surfer will be looking at the welcome page of the site he or she wanted to visit in the browser window.

The World Wide Web brings thousands of resources to our fingertips. Within a few hours, students can gather important and interesting details that would take days to collect using traditional sources.

Browser Basics

Not all browsers are created equal. Great researchers get to know a few different browsers because each has features that are exclusive to that browser. Common browsers include Safari, Internet Explorer, Netscape Navigator, Opera, AOL, Chrome, and Firefox.

Web pages are made with HTML (hypertext markup language) code, the computer's instructions behind the design and content of a page. The code creates neat features like background color, animations, and buttons. Each browser interprets the HTML code to produce the page, but it isn't always the same across browsers. A Web page may have certain features that will load only on certain browsers. Sometimes, this is on purpose and sometimes it's a glitch. Some commercial Web sites may insist that their site be viewed through a browser of their choice.

The wrong browser can also cause problems when requesting information. When filling out online forms or requests, researchers may find that they can't complete the process. Maybe they get to a certain stage and then an error message loads, or they are booted from the system. If the researcher tries another browser, he or she will likely find the process goes through without a glitch. When visiting a major site, such as a government, educational, museum, or foundation site, and a feature isn't loading in the browser, the researcher should always try another browser before giving up the search.

Most library research computers will have more than one browser so researchers won't hit a dead end even if a problem occurs. For home use, there are many free browsers that can be downloaded. Some sites may ask researchers to upgrade the current browser in order to see newer features. If the computer being used is not the researcher's own, he or she needs to ask permission from the owner or school before downloading any new applications or upgrades.

Certain electronic resources, such as digital library collections, may have custom-built browsers. This is because the information is kept on a private network. The information isn't accessible through the Web. If the local library has electronic collections on a private network, the savvy researcher will take some time to get to know the browser. Libraries offer classes and tutorials to learn how to best use custom-made applications. This way, the researcher will get all the necessary information for a top-notch essay. As well, these classes will share some neat research tricks. The browser is a powerful tool, but it can't tell the researcher where to go. Think of the browser as a doorway that the researcher must walk through, but once on the other side, where to go is all up to him or her.

Google founders Larry Page *(left)* and Sergey Brin stand in front of stacks of servers. Google is one of the world's most popular search engines.

Search Engines

The Web is like a spider's web. Every cross of the spider's silk represents a link and Web page. The Web casts outward to millions of links and millions of pages. There are numerous pages on the Web that are merely place-holders. There are also inactive sites. It would be impossible to know what all of these sites are without some sort of organization. As well, it would be impossible for researchers to find what they are looking for without the help of search engines.

A search engine is a system that searches the Web for information. The system uses Web robots, which are also known as bots, crawlers, and spiders. Bots are applications that run automatically. The bots crawl through the Web, updating links and copying what they find. Search engines index or put this information into categories. When the surfer is ready to find something about a topic, dozens of bots have already crawled through old and new sites. Dozens of search engines have indexed this information. They're just waiting for the researcher to come look.

Popular search engines include Google, Ask.com, Yahoo!, AltaVista, and Live. When the researcher visits these search sites and enters a keyword or name, the search engine returns tens, hundreds, or thousands of Web addresses. There are also metasearch engines. Metasearch engines search the search engines themselves. They return the top-ranking results from many search engines. By using a metasearch engine, the researcher is accessing several search engines at once. Metasearch engines include Excite, HotBot, info.com, and Dogpile.

While metasearch engines can take a look at many search engines, they are computer-based and automatic. Each metasearch engine follows its own instructions to retrieve information from other search engines. Some search for the most common results. This means that the researcher isn't getting a deep dive into each search engine but is just skimming what's popular. When using metasearch engines, it's best to use at least two for thorough researching. Then compare what each one finds. For the best results, a researcher should make sure to search with keywords that are unique to the topic. The searcher should scroll through more than one listing of results to make sure that he or she has reached far and wide.

Organizing Inquiries

Every budding writer must follow the instructions that the teacher provides for each project. The teacher may require that the researcher present notes along with the final report. It's always best to ask for examples of what is expected in notes and supporting materials.

It's important to keep a record of Web sources and collected data. Researchers should save files and electronic notes on storage devices such as discs or flash drives.

The next step is to create a list of questions about the topic that will be answered through the research. A summary or outline can emerge from the questions. Once the list, summary, or outline is made, research can begin. On the computer, the researcher should create a folder. Everything that is collected from online research for the essay should be stored in the folder. If the computer is not yours, it is good to create a burn folder and use a disk or storage device to collect the work.

Researchers have different styles. Some like to read online and select only a few facts and Web sites. Some like to gather many sites and facts at once and then read through them while offline. Whatever the case, the researcher needs to copy the URL of each and every Web site used for gathering facts. The section or contents of the page need to be linked to the Web site in supporting documents.

Atop every section that is cut and pasted, the researcher should label it with the source—for instance "Mayo Clinic, Topic: Acne." He or she should copy the URL from the Web browser address and paste it there as well. It's also important to type in the time and date that the material was found on the Web. Web sites can change overnight, so retrieval time is important.

A great way to manage large amounts of collected data is to highlight or underline the facts that will support the report. After all of the necessary sites have been visited and the data collected, it'll be easy for the researcher to scroll through the document and find the facts that he or she thought were worth using. All of the facts need to have the original source mentioned along with them, so keeping organized like this will save time.

If cutting and pasting highlighted facts into a rough outline or first draft essay, the researcher must cut and paste the link or source along with it. During the writing stage, the researcher might find that he or she needs a little more insight in relation to a found fact. Having the original source along with it will allow the researcher to quickly go back to the link or links. He or she will be able to reread the research and gain further support for the point of view. Anything that is cut and pasted from another source must have the source information along with it.

Organizing the Search

Depending on the approach to Web research, results can help or hinder the work. If the researcher does too broad a sweep of a subject, he or she will get thousands of results. Weeding through the results will take a lot of time. If the researcher does a specific sweep, he or she might miss some interesting details found outside of what is being researched. Finding a balance through organized researching is key.

The researcher should begin the research process by creating a brief summary or outline. When given a topic, the researcher should take a

There are great resources on the Web, such as the Mayo Clinic's site, for an essay on medical conditions. This site has its own search feature for deep dives into a topic.

moment to think about it before diving right into the Web. He or she should consider what is being asked. Is the researcher being asked to explain the details about a person, place, or event in a straightforward manner? This is a descriptive essay. The researcher would be searching for broadly known facts about the topic. Is the project to evaluate a person's life, a place, or event, and give an opinion? This is a persuasive essay. The researcher would be searching for any facts that would support the point of view. Is the project for comparing two concepts, highlighting similarities or differences? This is a comparative essay. The researcher will need to dig into both topics. The challenge will be keeping track of which details are similar and which are different per topic.

Once the researcher has evaluated what is being asked, a quick paragraph should be written about what he or she plans to do. The researcher should seek to explain why the essay is being written and what will hopefully be shared from the work. The next step is to think about any other topics or words that are related to the main topic. The researcher will want to keep these words in mind when doing a Web search. Once the search is done for the main topic, the search can be extended using combinations of topic-related words. Doing so will bring up other sites in case there is a need for more details than what was found with the main search.

Chapter 2

Primary Sources

Primary resources can be thought of as original sources. They are documents, illustrations, images, artifacts, or other items that come from the exact time of the topic's existence. They are produced by the subject's authorities or by someone with direct access to the subject. They can be produced well after an event, as long as the person recording the history was a witness.

For a topic that stems to current times, primary sources record important developments up through the present. Using the example of the volcano Mount Erebus, primary sources include documents and illustrations from the time of its discovery in the 1800s. Letters, graphs, maps, and any correspondence of the discoverer, Sir James Clark Ross, are also primary sources. Today, only scientists and support staff are allowed access to the volcano. Their scientific correspondence, maps, graphs, images, and artifacts are also primary sources. Every time an eruption or event occurs, the supporting documents and artifacts become part of the volcano's primary sources.

Responsible researchers and writers will always try to include the facts from at least one primary source. Primary sources can offer information that

File   Edit   View   Favorites   Tools   Help

NOT EVERYTHING IS TRUSTWORTHY

Not Everything Is Trustworthy

Even if accessing a site with lots of primary source information, the savvy researcher must be careful. Some foundations and organizations are formed to promote a certain idea to the public. They may not offer the complete story. They may offer materials that create a version of the truth but not the whole truth. The smart researcher approaches a site as if it must prove itself as valid before its facts can pass the test.

isn't repeated all across the Web. By digging deep, the researcher might be able to provide interesting information that his or her teacher or audience never knew. If the essay is able to teach something new, it goes from being an average essay to being a success.

Primary Sources Going Digital

In a big city, a researcher might be lucky enough to be near a major library. Many of these major libraries will have authentic primary sources in their special collections. Often, a patron must have special permission to see the original documents and artifacts. To make these incredibly historic items available to all of us, libraries rely upon computers. Many primary source items are digitized. They are copied, scanned, or photographed. The files are converted to accessible electronic formats like PDFs and JPEGs. This process of converting paper-based and hard-copy data into electronic data is known as digitization. Digitization can ensure that even if half a world away from a collection, a person can still access it.

Electronic and digital collections allow students to take an up-close look at documents they may never get to see in real life, such as the actual United States Constitution, Article 1.

Digital library collections are a great way to obtain access to primary sources. If blocked from a library's collections, the solution is to send an e-mail to the library. The researcher should explain that he or she is a student who is working on an essay and should include the topic. The librarian representative will explain how to access the digital library. If access is denied because it's a truly private collection, the librarian

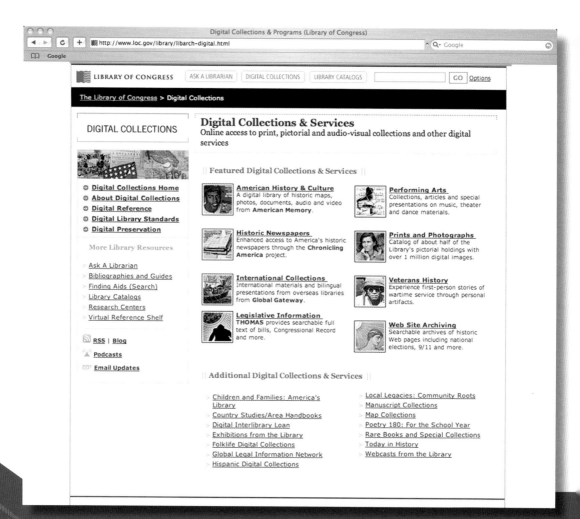

Collections such as the Library of Congress's Digital Collections portal have many features. One of these features includes asking a Library of Congress librarian a question directly.

representative may provide other alternatives. Students can also speak with the school librarian about the resources they're trying to access. The school librarian will strive to find an alternative or help locate the desired electronic files. To search for collections containing information about a historic person, for example, a researcher can use a search engine. The researcher would enter the name, and the word "library," "collection," or "exhibit."

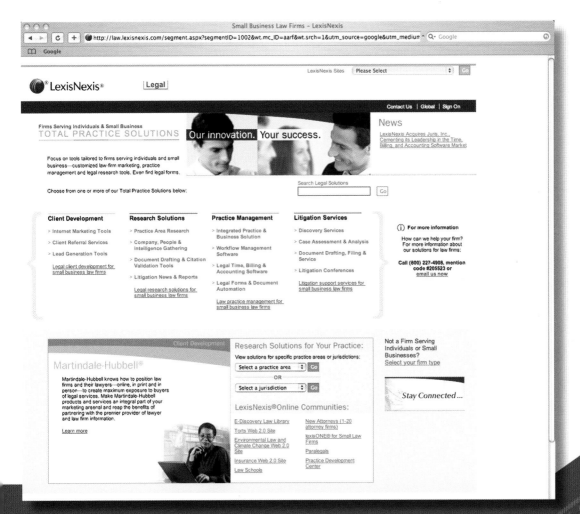

LexisNexis brings resources to thousands of customers. Its portal allows access to billions of documents from more than forty thousand legal, news, and business sources.

This will usually yield a few library-based Web sites about the person or related persons.

Any interviews with the subject or with key figures related to the subject are also considered primary sources. Most interviews are published in newspapers, journals, magazines, or books. LexisNexis offers a special kind of solution for accessing this information through the Web. It offers access to a variety of private sources, collections, news sources, journals, and magazines. Researchers can specify a range of dates from which they'd like to see articles. The service is so thorough that it'll pull up articles from every major and minor publication.

There are many different databases, for practically every major subject. Many libraries will subscribe to different databases if their own collections are not large. Subject-based databases include WHOLIS (the World Health Organization Library Database), which is great for health and medicine, and Anthropology Plus, which is great for news, articles, journals, and full texts on everything relating to anthropology. TRIS is a database from the U.S. Department of Transportation. It has over half a million records about research in the field of transportation. Oxford Art Online contains more than forty-five thousand articles about art.

In public and school libraries, databases allow further access to primary sources, including sources related to African American, women's, and presidential history. Researchers will be able to view historical maps, documents, and illustrations that they'd have to travel to see otherwise or that they wouldn't be allowed to see. Visitors might be asked to enter a library username and password to use the LexisNexis or Library Express network. The librarian representative will show anyone how to use the service. If it isn't found at a local school, it might be at the main public library.

MYTHS & FACTS

MYTH   Any government Web site can be trusted as reliable.

FACT   Some very controversial subjects between governments can cause sites to be biased. If there is a conflict between governments, it's best to visit government sites on both sides.

MYTH   Reliable information must be paid for.

FACT   Most information about a common topic is available for free somewhere in the world. Avoid paying for any information before doing a thorough search for it. The type of essays in school will be on topics where information is readily available and free.

MYTH   The newest information comes from the Web.

FACT   Not all information is up to date on the Web, even at government and academic sites. If the topic relies on the latest information, the researcher must make sure that the information is current.

Chapter 3

Secondary Sources

Although they are different from primary sources, secondary sources actually stem from primary sources. They are typically articles, studies, books, essays, and reports that discuss information from primary sources. Many secondary sources seek to tie up loose ends that weren't provided in primary sources. Secondary sources are created to provide further insight on a subject. They interpret whatever primary sources are available. They rely on what's known or believed. They may explore surfacing rumors or uncovered details. Secondary sources include magazine, newspaper, and journal articles; critiques and essays; and books.

Sometimes, a third type of source is available. Called tertiary sources, these are where primary and secondary resources are collected in one place. The third source includes manuals, textbooks, fact books, almanacs, encyclopedias, and guidebooks.

An easy way to explain all three types is by using the example of the topic of Martin Luther King Jr. There are letters by him, which are primary sources. The Nobel Foundation, which awards the Nobel Prize, has a Web page on him. This is a secondary source. There are also biographies, or

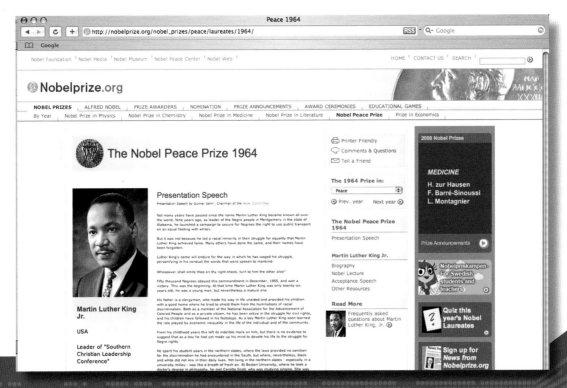

Nobelprize.org is the official Web site of the Nobel Foundation. This entry on Martin Luther King Jr. includes a biography, a frequently asked questions section, and his acceptance speech after winning the Nobel Prize.

books about his life, which are secondary sources. Now if someone wants to create an encyclopedia of the civil rights movement, the publisher will use passages from his letters and even include information obtained from the Nobel Foundation Web site. All of these sources are pulled together in the tertiary source encyclopedia.

Double-Check the Facts

When surfing a commercial site for facts, the source must be evaluated. Most information about the owner of a Web site can be found by navigating

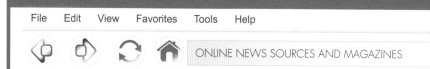

File   Edit   View   Favorites   Tools   Help

ONLINE NEWS SOURCES AND MAGAZINES

Online News Sources and Magazines

We live in a world of media conglomerates. There are a lot of huge companies that own dozens of smaller companies. Large broadcast companies own a lot of smaller news and media sources. If the controlling company has certain political ideas, those ideas may filter to its news outlets. This means the news may be biased in favor of the company's opinions. As well, sometimes what these companies deem as news is really a marketing campaign to push products, stars, or ideas. This means that when we find interviews with our subject, we may not find entire interviews. Certain quotes might be edited to produce a bias.

Quotes can be manipulated to make a person appear a certain way. The savvy researcher tries to track down the entire interview rather than pieces of it. These pieces are known as excerpts. Often, news sources will offer the entire interview through transcripts. The researcher will locate the transcript link on the same page where the article is found. If there isn't one, the author's or interviewer's e-mail address may be available. A copy of the complete interview or a link to where it can be found can be requested from the author or interviewer. A copy might also be obtained through the contact section of the site if there is one.

The "About Us" section of most Web sites offers valuable information about the source. Time Warner's "About Us" page shows its relationship to other giants, such as AOL, Turner Broadcasting, and HBO.

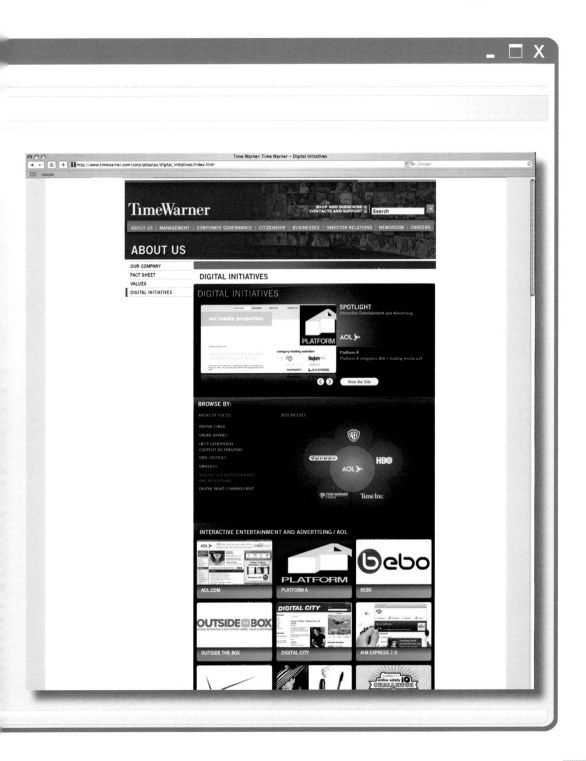

to the "About" section or "History" section if there is one. The researcher should see whether the statement includes something like "strive to bring fair and impartial news to the public." This will let the researcher know that at the very least, being impartial is a concern of the Web site.

If a researcher is at a biased site anyway and the facts are great, he or she can use them. The researcher just needs to make sure that the facts can be found in other sources. If the facts can be found on a government, educational, museum, or foundation site, he or she is good to go. Search engines bring up all kinds of these sites. There is a quick way to identify types of sites. This is by the last three letters after the last period in the URL:

Local government sites are great Web sources. Local sites offer daily articles about hot topics and have links to archived resources, such as on the government Web site for New York City.

.com: A commercial or company site; sometimes an individual's site
.net: A commercial/company site or individual's site
.gov: A site funded or operated by the government
.edu: An academic site, such as a university library or collection
.org: An organization's, foundation's, or museum's site; can also be an individual's site

There aren't strict laws that make an individual or company stick to a particular address. At least with .gov and .edu sites, the researcher knows that it's completely a government or academic source. These are relatively

Anyone can register a domain name and create a Web site. Companies such as Network Solutions allow you to buy a unique domain name for a reasonable price.

trustworthy because creating, posting, and modifying content on these sites is done only by government or academic professionals. These are great sites to validate or double-check the facts found at news, broadcast, or media sites.

Let's take the example of a researcher studying STDs among teens. The researcher found a statistic that says one out of every four teens will get an STD. The statistic was found on a blog. A blog is a personal publishing page, often filled with timely articles relating to the news. Anyone can be a blogger, and a blogger can write about anything. Many companies use blogs, too, so blogs can be commercial as well. The blogger says he found the STD statistic at the American Social Health Association Web site. The researcher clicks the link and it takes him or her to the association's Web

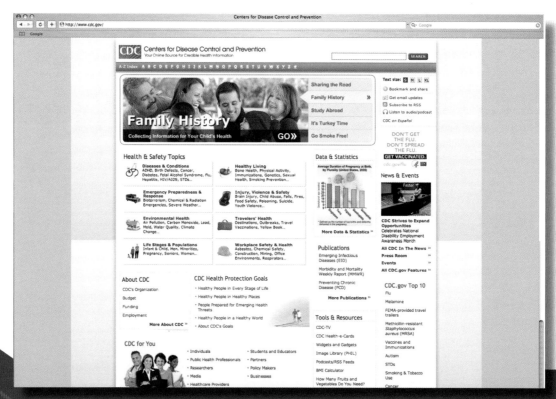

Trusted government Web sites, such as that of the Centers for Disease Control and Prevention, bring together hundreds of resources for the latest information on important topics, such as health.

page. While it's a great (but scary) statistic for the essay, the association doesn't say where the statistic comes from. Now what? The researcher can't cite the blogger because it's not his study or findings; he's merely reporting someone else's information.

The researcher has two choices. One, the researcher can just use the American Social Health Association Web site and cite it as the source. Two, the researcher can take the professional step of validating the fact by searching elsewhere for it. If the researcher chooses option one, it's OK, but he or she is not going to have a strong source-based essay. Choice two provides support for the fact or shows how the fact was wrong.

The researcher's next step is to go to the search engine and enter "one out of four teens will get an STD," or similar language. What comes up is surprising. There are a lot of links that say one out of four teenage girls have an STD. The CDC, which is the authoritative Centers for Disease Control and Prevention (a government agency), is mentioned, too. The researcher goes to www.cdc.gov and types "STD teenage girls" in the search field.

The first result is a timely press release. The findings were that one in every four teenage girls has an STD. Now the fact has its source and it's in its correct form. It also leads the researcher to consider other questions, such as why the statistic is solely about girls and not all teens? The simple process of validation can lead to further questions to answer in the essay.

Chapter 4

Cyber Code of Ethics

Before the Web, data was found in the paper world of books, journals, and magazines. Students had to photocopy the copyright page of the material, the page—or section—where the information was found, and the bibliography or sources section. They then typed the statistics and facts they wanted to use. Then they cited the source at the end of their essay or within footnotes. The photocopies were highlighted, stored, and saved for backup in case a teacher questioned the facts. If photocopies weren't available, the student had to handwrite or type all this information as backup.

If the teacher requests that a researcher use print and hard copy sources, the researcher will either need to keep excellent handwritten or typed notes, or create photocopies of the sources that may be used. The researcher should maintain a go-to list of all sources. The sources need to be numbered, as well as linked to the corresponding notes or photocopies. Because the researcher will be using supporting information from these sources, he or she must take time to read and understand the material. Some resources cannot be checked out of the library, so it's important to "get" the material up front to be able to

When writing directly from printed sources, make sure to photocopy the sections used and always document where the printed source came from.

write about it later. As well, it'll allow the researcher to highlight only important supporting facts rather than taking many pages of notes or photocopies. If more than one library or collection is used, the researcher should make a list of where the sources were obtained in the library.

With electronic media and portable laptops, the copy and paste options have become daily tools. We can quickly copy and paste a URL, a paragraph of text, the source, and entire sections of material. We can drag and drop images into a report within seconds. We can keep entire sections of research in an electronic document that we can pull up anytime, day or night. With ease comes speed, but also mistakes. There are dangers associated with having it all at our fingertips. Researchers can easily forget where information comes from, or can even mistake someone else's work for their own. After

Track the date and time you access information from any Web site. Content can change rapidly, such as on the White House Web site (http://www.whitehouse.gov), which displays the latest news.

becoming pros at tracking down real facts, researchers need to make sure they know how to manage them properly.

Citing Sources

Everything and anything a researcher obtains from another source must be cited. A fact is useless to the essay unless it can be linked to a source. There are good habits to get into to ensure that facts are being managed correctly. For example, a teacher asks a student to write an essay on the rebuilding of Louisiana after Hurricane Katrina. The White House's Web site states, "Significant progress has been made in the region." The researcher can cut and paste the quote from the Web page into the essay. However,

n children's books . . . Genuinely funny, the s a marvelously human portrait of an e adolescent."[8] A review for the *School 'ournal*, stated that "Lowry has the ability to : common experiences and situations in an on and [lively] manner, while at the same oviding easy access for readers who will edly find that many of Anastasia's notions lose relation to their own."[9]

When attributing a source, place a number (called a superscript) outside of the quoted material. The attribution relates to a source list that explains where the information came from.

the researcher must get in the habit of immediately copying the URL and date of the article into a list of sources. It's easy if there is a separate document open where the information can be drop into. He or she then numbers the facts that were pasted into the essay. The researcher needs to make sure the number relates to the source that was pasted into the list. The researcher copies and pastes the date of the article and the author's name. He or she can copy and paste the owner or company if there isn't an author. If there isn't an article date, the researcher can copy or type the Web site's copyright date.

Now the researcher can get back to writing. He or she could write, for example, "According to the White House, 'significant progress has been made in the region.'" The researcher can also drop it next to his or her own words without mentioning the White House. If so, the researcher must use quotes. For example: "Changes are noticeable, and 'significant progress has been made in the region.'"[6] The source note "6" corresponds to the footnotes or the bibliography. That's where the source information that was copied and pasted earlier will be placed. The teacher will tell students which form of citation is preferred. No matter what type is preferred, students must always keep the source details linked to the facts in some organizational way. It's truly annoying to lose a juicy fact because where it came from was forgotten or the source can't be found again.

Researching Dangers

As the researcher navigates through dozens of Web sites, he or she is learning about the topic. It's important to try to keep track of what is already known versus what is being learned through research. Sometimes the way something is said might strike a chord with the reader. It's important to analyze why what is said is liked. It's equally important not to memorize it because this can lead to problems. Plagiarism, or copying someone else's work or idea and passing it off as one's own, can happen accidentally or on purpose.

The researcher might like the way a Web site explains an idea. He or she innocently tries to remember it so it can be revisited or reworked later

Teachers are very familiar with the topics that they assign. They can easily spot plagiarism. A responsible researcher is careful to make sure that all borrowed material is clearly identified with citations.

during the writing. While writing away, the information just flows as the researcher is typing. The researcher might just have accidentally repeated what was read earlier, which is someone else's work.

Sometimes, ideas or text just aren't coming and the researcher sees it expressed well somewhere. "What's the problem with one little sentence from somewhere else?" he or she may wonder. The researcher copies and pastes, and there it is—instant essay. It's not original text, though. Researchers beware; every teacher has read hundreds of essays. They will be able to recognize in an instant writing that belongs to the student versus text that belongs to

File   Edit   View   Favorites   Tools   Help

AVOID BIAS

Avoid Bias

Another danger for researchers is wanting their opinion to prevail no matter what the research supports. It's necessary to have a point of view in the essay. Even if the goal is just to share information, it's a point of view. Sometimes, the point of view we start out with gets voided out by the facts. Sometimes, a lack of facts leaves us scratching our heads. The researcher may find that fact after fact is bullying against his or her opinion. Maybe there are glimmers of hope here and there, but what is being found isn't very supportive.

Researchers, even scientific researchers, have been guilty in the past of altering results. They want a specific end, so they shape all findings to produce that end. They look for only the facts that will support their desired result. The same can happen as students gather facts. Sometimes it's knowingly and sometimes it isn't. The first time a researcher finds a fact that goes against his or her goals, the researcher needs to stop and take a break. He or she needs to think about the fact and the source. Is it trusted? If so, then how is it opposing his or her view? Does the fact make sense? If so, then how did the researcher develop his or her view that is in opposition to this fact?

someone else. One little copied sentence can turn any essay into a failure. The savvy researcher wants to avoid plagiarizing anything at all costs.

Finishing Up

It's good to take just an hour or so and recreationally read about the topic. Researchers should read about their topics as if they aren't writing a report,

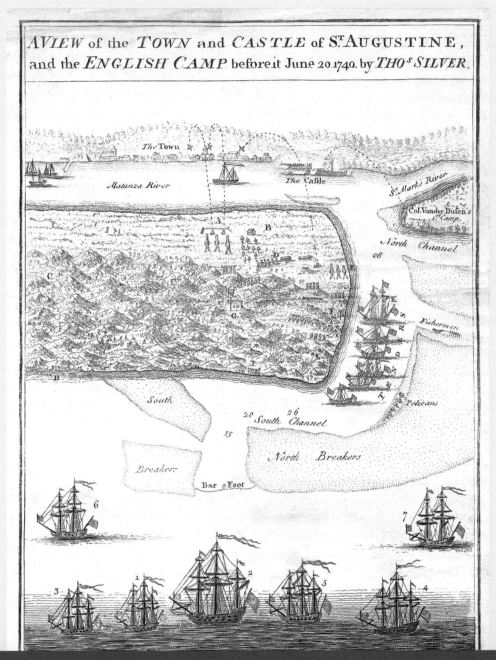

A VIEW of the TOWN and CASTLE of St. AUGUSTINE, and the ENGLISH CAMP before it June 20.1740. by THOs SILVER.

A world of interesting primary and secondary resources, such as this map from 1740, awaits the budding researcher turned writer.

but for fun. They should let ideas form in their minds around what is being read. They may find the essay's topic is changing slightly—or greatly. Great researchers don't stay stubbornly attached to the original essay idea. They simply change the essay and let the teacher know what happened. A teacher will probably tell his or her students that some of the greatest essays were led by the facts. The savvy researcher resists all urges to reinterpret facts to suit his or her needs. This is using resources carelessly. When a researcher does this, real pros can disprove almost any work.

Last, the budding researcher is standing on the shoulders of other researchers and writers. Researchers must always ask permission to use materials if they aren't sure they're allowed to. Citing where information comes from is not only a responsibility but a sign of respect. The owner or creator of any images, maps, or graphs must be credited if the work is used to support an essay. A well-researched and well-written essay can live long past its purpose of getting a grade. Teachers might keep top papers as examples. Top papers might spawn larger group projects or further studies. The researcher, when following the rules, can create an essay that lasts and is remembered, and is maybe even quoted by future researchers.

TEN GREAT QUESTIONS

TO ASK A LIBRARIAN

1 What magazine, book, and video resources do you have here that can introduce the topic?

2 Do you have any primary source book collections?

3 Do you have access to any digital primary or secondary source collections?

4 Do you have LexisNexis, Library Express, or a database with old and new articles, journals, and magazines?

5 What electronic collections do you have access to on the Web from here?

6 Do you have tutorials or classes on research and writing?

7 Can you get into the city's public library electronic database and collections from this computer?

8 Do you have access to any university collections?

9 Where is information that is out of the ordinary for this topic found?

10 What's most interesting to you about this topic?

GLOSSARY

biased Unfair preference or dislike of something.

blog A Web page or pages that serve as a personal or commercial journal.

browser An application that allows the user to surf the Web. Popular browsers include Safari, Internet Explorer, Netscape Navigator, Opera, AOL, and Firefox.

citation A quotation from a source.

cite To give credit to a source.

comparative essay An essay that explores two or more topics.

controversial Provoking strong disagreement.

descriptive essay An essay that describes people, places, or things in a straightforward manner.

excerpt A passage or section taken from a larger whole.

HTML Hypertext markup language; code or instructions for Web-based applications.

infinite Limitless or very great in size.

meta Beyond or more developed.

metasearch engine Massive search system that searches search engines. Examples include Excite, HotBot, info.com, and Dogpile.

persuasive essay An essay that offers a factually supported opinion about a person, place, or event.

plagiarism Copying someone else's work or idea and passing it off as your own.

primary sources Original documents, illustrations, photographs, artifacts, video, audio, and interviews that provide firsthand information about a topic.

search engine A system that searches the Web for information.

secondary sources Sources that interpret whatever primary sources are available. Includes magazine, newspaper, and journal articles; critiques and essays; and books.

tertiary sources Sources where primary and secondary resources are collected. Includes manuals, textbooks, fact books, almanacs, encyclopedias, and guidebooks.

transcript A complete written record of something.

unsubstantiated Not proven factually.

URL Uniform resource locator; an address that identifies a file on the Web.

validate To confirm or establish the truthfulness or accuracy of something.

American Library Association
50 East Huron
Chicago, IL 60611
(800) 545-2433
Web site: http://www.ala.org
The American Library Association (ALA) strives to bring excellence and
    guidance to school librarians across the United States. The ALA's site
    offers KC (KidsConnect). This section has tips and tools to help you
    become more familiar and comfortable with the research process.

Library of Congress
101 Independence Avenue SE
Washington, DC 20540-1400
(202) 707-9779
Web site: http://www.loc.gov
The Library of Congress serves as the research center for the U.S. Congress.
    Its Web site offers access to thousands of important primary source
    documents, images, and files. The Library of Congress is the largest
    library in the world.

National Archives and Records Administration
8601 Adelphi Road
College Park, MD 20740-6001
(866) 272-6272
Web site: http://www.archives.gov
The National Archives and Records Administration huge archive collects
    and manages important (and daily) documents created and used by
    the U.S. federal government.

Natural Resources Canada: The Atlas of Canada
615 Booth Street, Room 650
Ottawa, ON K1A 0E9
Canada
(613) 995-0947
(613) 996-4397 (hearing-impaired)
E-mail: info@atlas.gc.ca
Web site: http://atlas.nrcan.gc.ca/site/english/index.html
Natural Resources Canada is Canada's official resource of maps and
    historical documents.

Statistics Canada Learning Resources
150 Tunney's Pasture Driveway
Ottawa, ON K1A 0T6
Canada
Web site: http://www.statcan.ca/english/edu/students.htm
Statistics Canada Learning Resources is Canada's national statistic agency. It
    offers numerous resources for learning (and teaching) in school.

Web Sites

Due to the changing nature of Internet links, Rosen Publishing has developed
an online list of Web sites related to the subject of this book. This site is
updated regularly. Please use this link to access the list:

http://www.rosenlinks.com/dil/rppe

FOR FURTHER READING

Chin, Beverly, ed. *How to Write a Great Research Paper*. Hoboken, NJ: John Wiley & Sons, Inc., 2004.

Flash Kids Editors. *Fearless Writing: Essay Workbook* (Flash Kids Fearless). New York, NY: Spark Publishing, 2007.

Flash Kids Editors. *Fearless Writing: Research Paper Workbook* (Flash Kids Fearless). New York, NY: Spark Publishing, 2007.

Hallinan, Camilla, ed. *Online Encyclopedia*. New York, NY: DK Publishing, Inc., 2006.

Hawthorne, Kate, and Daniela Sheppard. *The Young Person's Guide to the Internet: An Essential Web Site Reference Book for Young People, Parents, and Teachers*. Florence, KY: Routledge, 2005.

Janeczko, Paul B. *Writing Winning Reports and Essays* (Scholastic Guides). New York, NY: Scholastic, Inc., 2003.

Nicholson, Sue, and Fran Baines, et al., eds. *E.Encyclopedia*. New York, NY: DK Publishing, Inc., 2003.

Souter, Gerry, Janet Souter, and Allison Souter. *Researching on the Internet Using Search Engines, Bulletin Boards, and Listservs*. Berkeley Heights, NJ: Enslow Publishers, Inc., 2003.

Wolinsky, Art. *Internet Power Research Using the Big Approach*. Rev. ed. Berkeley Heights, NJ: Enslow Publishers, Inc., 2005.

American Library Association. "Using Primary Sources." 2008. Retrieved September 5, 2008 (http://www.ala.org/ala/mgrps/divs/rusa/ rusaourassoc/rusasections/historysection/histsect/histcomm/ instructionres/usingprimarysources.cfm).

Gibaldi, Phyllis Franklin. *MLA Handbook for Writers of Research Papers.* 6th ed. New York, NY: Modern Language Association of America, 2003.

Mann, Thomas. *The Oxford Guide to Library Research.* New York, NY: Oxford University Press, 1998.

Netcraft Internet Services. "August 2008 Web Server Survey." Retrieved September 9, 2008 (http://news.netcraft.com/archives/Web_ server_survey.html).

Public Broadcasting Systems. "Media Giants." 1995–2008. Retrieved September 5, 2008 (http://www.pbs.org/wgbh/pages/frontline/ shows/cool/giants).

Quinn, Stephen, and Stephen Lamble. *Online Newsgathering: Research and Reporting for Journalism.* St. Louis, MO: Focal Press, 2007.

Schlein, Alan. *Find It Online: The Complete Guide to Online Research.* 4th ed. Tempe, AZ: Facts on Demand Press, 2004.

Turabain, Kate, Wane C. Booth, and University of Chicago Press Staff. *A Manual for Writers of Research Papers, Theses, and Dissertations: Chicago Style for Students and Researchers.* Rev. ed. Chicago, IL: University of Chicago Press, 2007.

INDEX

About the Author

Holly Cefrey is an award-winning children's author. She has worked as a fact-checker for print and digital organizations. She enjoys surfing, searching, and exploring the Web, both for information and for fun.

Photo Credits

Cover, p. 1 (top left), p. 11 © www.shutterstock.com; cover, p. 1 (top right), p. 17 OurDocuments.gov; p. 7 © Fred de Noyelle/Godong/Corbis; p. 9 © Kim Kullah/Corbis; p. 31 © www.istockphoto.com/Bart Coenders; p. 35 © Spencer Grant/Photo Edit; p. 38 Ed Jackson.

Designer: Nicole Russo; Editor: Nicholas Croce;
Photo Researcher: Marty Levick

EAGLE PUBLIC LIBRARY DIST.
BOX 240 EAGLE, CO 81631
(970) 328-8800